I didn't know that quakes split the ground open

© Aladdin Books Ltd 1999
Produced by
Aladdin Books Ltd
28 Percy Street
London W1P 0LD

First published in the United States in 1999 by
Copper Beech Books,
an imprint of
The Millbrook Press
2 Old New Milford Road
Brookfield, Connecticut 06804

Concept, editorial, and design by
David West Children's Books

Designer: Flick Killerby
Illustrators: Peter Roberts — Allied Artists,
Jo Moore, Graham Kennedy — Allied Artists

Printed in Belgium

Cataloging-in-Publication Data is on file
at the Library of Congress.

ISBN 0-7613-0912-8 (lib.bdg.)
ISBN 0-7613-0795-8 (trade)

5 4 3 2 1

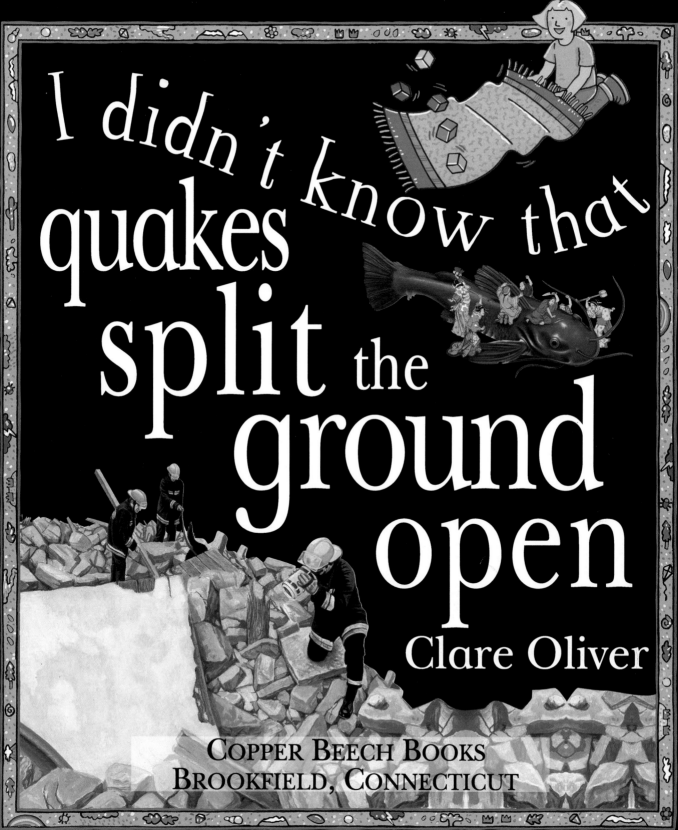

I didn't know that
quakes split the ground open

Clare Oliver

COPPER BEECH BOOKS
BROOKFIELD, CONNECTICUT

I didn't know that

Introduction

Did *you* know that there are over a million earthquakes every year? ... that roads and bridges can be snapped in two? ... that

earthquakes under the sea cause tidal waves?

Discover for yourself amazing facts about earthquakes and the devastation they can cause. Learn how to predict them, and find out what to do if you get caught in one.

 Watch for this symbol that means there is a fun project for you to try.

 Is it true or is it false? Watch for this symbol and try to answer the question before reading on for the answer.

Don't forget to check the borders for extra amazing facts.

The longest-ever recorded quake lasted four minutes in Alaska in 1964. The ocean bed was shaken up and down, causing a 30-foot-high wall of water to hit the coast.

I didn't know that

quakes split the ground open. The ground beneath your feet may feel firm, but it's not! Sometimes strains build up under the surface, the ground rumbles, and the solid rock cracks apart. This is called a tremor or, if it's big, an earthquake.

6

A big quake struck Afghanistan in 1998. Many people's remote homes were destroyed so they had to resettle elsewhere.

True or false?
An earthquake at night is called a moonquake.

Answer: **False**
A moonquake is a tremor on the moon. Sometimes pieces of space rock, called *meteorites*, smash into the moon and make the ground shake.

There are over a million earthquakes every year; some are tiny.

I didn't know that

waves travel through land.

The earth's surface is covered in *plates* that constantly push against each other. When the plates move apart, shock waves are sent through the land. You can't see shock waves but you can feel them.

Most earthquakes happen along *fault* lines where the rocks are weak and where two or more plates meet.

SEARCH & FIND
Can you find four cars?
FIND & SEARCH

Epicenter

Fault

The shock waves start deep underground, at the *focus* of the pressure between the plates. The place where these waves hit the surface will be the earthquake's center, which scientists call the *epicenter*.

Focus

rocked skyscrapers in Texas.

Plates start
to move.

Quake
occurs.

The pressure can build up for centuries, but eventually — snap! — the plates shift. The pressure escapes in the form of shock waves that ripple outward from the quake's focus.

See what happens when one of the earth's plates shifts. For the earth's plate, use a rug. Add some buildings: small boxes will do. Pull one end of the rug sharply to move the "plate." What happens to the boxes?

A quake's first shock waves are called body waves.

On the San Andreas Fault, in California, beams of laser light shine across the fault. If a section of earth slips a tiny bit, detectors on the other side measure the slippage.

I didn't know that dragons and toads sense quakes. This bronze pot (right) was the first quake detector. In a tremor, a dragon would drop its ball into a toad's mouth. By seeing which toad held a ball, the inventor knew where the quake was starting.

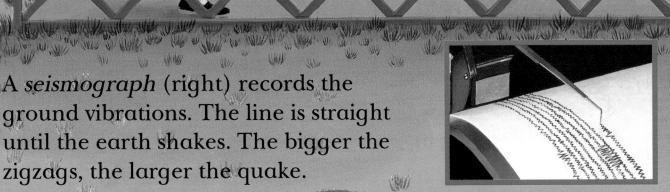

A *seismograph* (right) records the ground vibrations. The line is straight until the earth shakes. The bigger the zigzags, the larger the quake.

 True or false?
A *creepmeter* measures the length of the slimy trail a snail makes.

Answer: **False**
It is an underground machine that measures how much the earth's plates shift, or creep.

The Chinese thought when rabbits panicked, an earthquake was coming.

I didn't know that

earthquakes ring bells.

Scientists number earthquakes to show their strength. The Richter scale grades the strength of an earthquake from 0-9 using seismograph readings. A quake that makes a church bell ring is grade 4 on the Richter scale.

The *Mercalli scale* (right) grades quakes from I (one) to XII (twelve). A grade IV (four) quake causes the same sort of shaking as a heavy truck passing.

1 EARTHQUAKE FELT BY INSTRUMENTS AND ONLY A FEW PEOPLE.

4. FELT INDOORS LIKE PASSING OF HEAVY TRUCKS. DISHES AND WINDOWS RATTLE.

7. FELT BY DRIVERS. WAVES ON PONDS. DIFFICULT TO STAND.

CHIMNEYS AN MONUMENTS COLLAPSE.

11. FEW BUILDINGS LEFT STANDING. BRIDGES AND UNDERGROUND PIPES DESTROYED. CRACKS IN THE GROUND.

Mercalli based his scale on what quake victims reported.

2. FELT ON UPPER FLOORS BY PEOPLE RESTING.

3. FELT INDOORS, ESPECIALLY UPSTAIRS. PARKED CARS MAY SWAY.

5. MANY WAKENED. PLASTER CRACKS.

6. MANY RUN OUTSIDE, MOVING FURNITURE. CHURCH BELLS RING.

9. CRACKS IN ROADS.

10. LANDSLIDES. RIVERS OVERFLOW.

12. DEVASTATION. GROUND WAVES LIKE THE SEA.

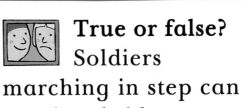 **True or false?** Soldiers marching in step can topple a bridge.

Answer: **True**

Soldiers break step when crossing small bridges. If they marched in step, the bridge might bounce and break! Many bridges shake, topple, and break under a quake's pressure.

SEARCH & FIND SEARCH & FIND

Can you find four dogs?

13

I didn't know that

quakes topple bridges.

When a big quake struck Northridge, California, in 1994 three roads were closed as ten supporting bridges collapsed. The quake measured between VIII (eight) and IX (nine) on the Mercalli scale.

Quakes that hit cities cause most damage, as expensive bridges, roads, and buildings must be rebuilt. In 1995 a quake shifted the city of Kobe in Japan 5.6 feet. Two thousand feet of highway toppled sideways.

The Northridge quake was the costliest U.S. natural disaster ever.

A powerful earthquake can twist solid metal train tracks as if they were pipe cleaners. This happened in Kobe, Japan, in 1995.

SEARCH & FIND

Can you find the missing road section?

FIND & SEARCH

SEARCH & FIND
Can you find the stretcher-bearers?
FIND & SEARCH & FIND & SEARCH

To see how quakes affect swampy land, fill one deep tray with dry sand and another with wet sand. Place a "building" in each tray. Bang on the table. The building in the wet sand will sink farther.

A 1985 quake had its epicenter in Michoacán, Mexico, where the ground is rock solid.

I didn't know that houses can sink. The quake in Michoacán caused more damage 236 miles away in Mexico City than it did on the rocky land of Michoacán.

In 1989, wooden buildings in San Francisco slipped off their foundations and sank during an earthquake. The ground beneath them was not very solid.

Mexico City is built on a dried-up, swampy lake.

True or false?
Before a quake, ponds get extra smelly.

Answer: **True**

As the pressure under the ground builds up, gases build up too and leak into groundwater, which is the water just below land level, and pond water. Some of these gases smell.

Animals can become jumpy just before a quake. It's as if they know what is about to happen.

I didn't know that

a table can save your life. One of the biggest quake dangers is being hit on the head. Find something to protect your head, then crouch under a sturdy table. Another safe place to stand is in a doorway.

The film *Earthquake* told the story of a big tremor hitting Los Angeles. Everyone who lives there in real life has to be prepared in case a "Big One" strikes.

Gases in the ground often make quake fires so hot they can melt glass.

In 1970 an earthquake caused one of the worst landslides ever. The shock waves dislodged ice on the Andes, which turned into a *mudflow* that swept away the town of Yungay, Peru, killing 50,000.

SEARCH & FIND
Can you find three rooftops?
FIND & SEARCH

The Yungay landslide was 260 feet high.

True or false?
Earthquakes make mud boil.

Answer: **True**
A quake's shock waves can make mud spurt up in 12-inch cones, or *sand boils.*

I didn't know that

you can drown in mud. Sometimes, the aftereffects of an earthquake are more dangerous than the quake itself. When a quake shakes ice from mountain peaks, the ice melts and runs downward. As it flows it gathers pieces of earth and rock. The mudflow can move fast enough to sweep away people, cars, and houses.

I didn't know that

waves wash away cities. When an earthquake strikes at sea, the trembling seabed churns up monster waves. In 1755 a quake 200 miles out to sea from Lisbon, Portugal, created a huge tidal wave that destroyed the city's buildings.

Can you find the donkey?

SEARCH & FIND & FIND SEARCH &

True or false?
A tidal wave is called a *tsunami.*

Answer: **True**
"Tsunami" is the proper word to use. It's a Japanese word that means "harbor wave." Japan gets hit by many tsunamis from the Pacific.

22

In 1992 an earthquake rumbled out at sea off the coast of Nicaragua, Central America. The quake made 50-foot-high waves — over ten times as tall as you — and wrecked 190 miles of coast.

True or false?
Eight elephants hold up the world.

Answer: **True**

True, if you believe the ancient Hindu myth that the earth rests on eight elephants. When an elephant shakes its head, there is an earthquake.

The ancient Mongolians thought a giant frog held up the earth.

The ancient Greeks believed a huge bull lived under the palace at Knossos, Crete, and that its bellowing shook the earth. Knossos was flattened by a quake 3,400 years ago.

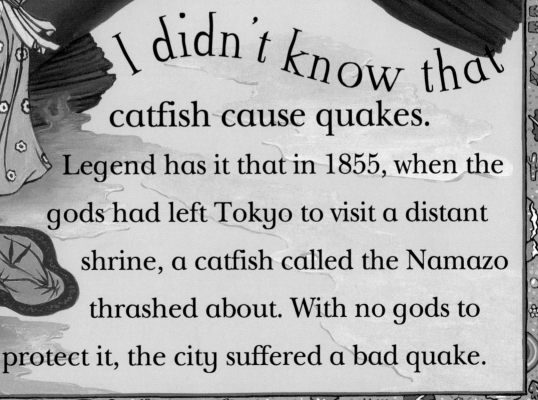

I didn't know that

catfish cause quakes.

Legend has it that in 1855, when the gods had left Tokyo to visit a distant shrine, a catfish called the Namazo thrashed about. With no gods to protect it, the city suffered a bad quake.

After an earthquake, rescue workers need special equipment for finding trapped victims. *Infrared cameras* can "see" body heat through many layers of rubble. With the help of these, rescuers know where to start digging first.

SEARCH & FIND
Can you find three rescue dogs?
FIND & SEARCH

Japan has an annual National Disaster Prevention Day on the anniversary of the 1923 Tokyo earthquake. People practice what to do in a quake. Children wear fireproof capes (right).

26

I didn't know that

dogs rescue quake victims.

Sniffer dogs are used to search for victims. They are specially trained for the job. With their sensitive noses, the dogs can smell where people are lying beneath rubble.

 True or false?

The worst quake this century killed 750,000 people.

Answer: **Don't know**
Some say 750,000 died at T'ang-shan, China, in 1976. But the official figure is just under 250,000.

! People who flock to see an earthquake are called "disaster tourists."

True or false?

Houses were made of paper.

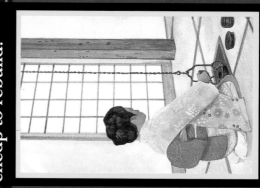

Answer: **True**

In Japan some houses were built of paper and balsa wood: easy and cheap to rebuild!

I didn't know that

pyramid-shaped buildings are very strong. The San Francisco Transamerica Building is wider at the bottom than at the top, and so has a sturdier base to withstand tremors.

Use building blocks to test how sturdy different shapes are when you make the table shake. A shape that is wider at the top than at the bottom is the most unstable.

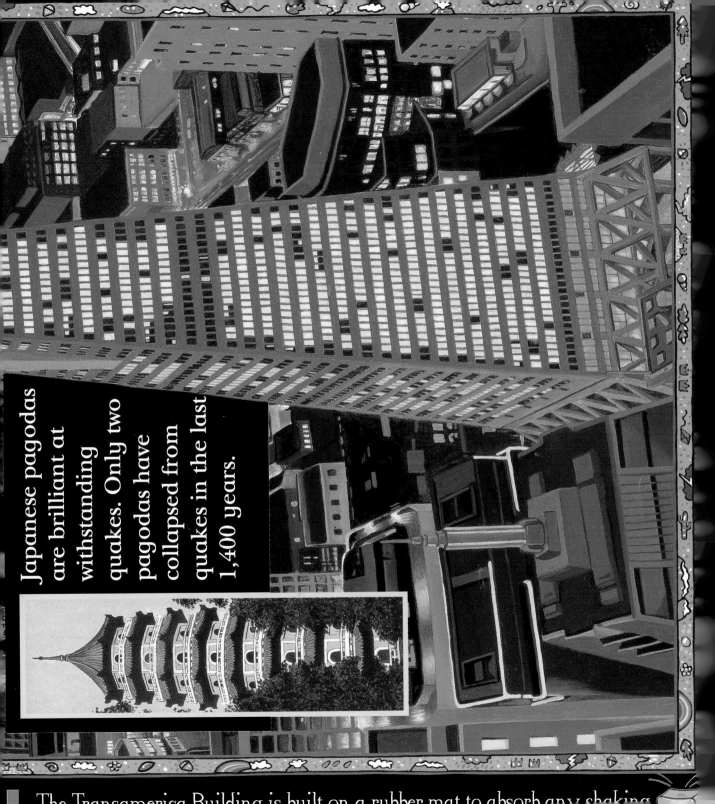

Japanese pagodas are brilliant at withstanding quakes. Only two pagodas have collapsed from quakes in the last 1,400 years.

The Transamerica Building is built on a rubber mat to absorb any shaking.

Glossary

Creepmeter
A machine that measures "creep," that is, how far each year the earth's plates move.

Epicenter
The center of an earthquake on the ground.

Fault
A crack in the rocks that form the earth's surface.

Focus
The starting point of an earthquake underground.

Infrared camera
A camera that shows up any hot areas, for example, body heat, as red. It can see right "through" darkness or rubble.

Mercalli scale
A range of numbers that describes how powerful an earthquake is, based on what witnesses of the quake saw.

Meteorite
Space rock that has broken away from a comet's fiery tail and smashes into a planet or moon.

Mudflow

A "river" of rock, earth, and water that can start out when an ice-covered mountain peak is shaken and melted in an earthquake.

Plates

Large sections of the earth's crust that are constantly moving against each other.

Sand boil

Cone-shaped peaks of bubbling mud, created by earthquakes.

Seismograph

A machine that measures the force of an earthquake. A printout from the machine is called a seismogram.

Tsunami

A giant wave, caused by an earthquake or a volcanic eruption.

Index